Visions of Him

Seeing God in Everyday Things

ROBYN BESEMANN

WESTBOW°
PRESS
A DIVISION OF THOMAS NELSON
& ZONDERVAN

Scripture taken from the Holy Bible, NEW INTERNATIONAL VERSION®. Copyright © 1973, 1978, 1984 by Biblica, Inc. All rights reserved worldwide. Used by permission. NEW INTERNATIONAL VERSION® and NIV® are registered trademarks of Biblica, Inc. Use of either trademark for the offering of goods or services requires the prior written consent of Biblica US, Inc.

WestBow Press books may be ordered through booksellers or by contacting:

WestBow Press
A Division of Thomas Nelson & Zondervan
1663 Liberty Drive
Bloomington, IN 47403
www.westbowpress.com
1 (866) 928-1240

ISBN: 978-1-4908-8404-2 (sc)
ISBN: 978-1-4908-8403-5 (e)

Library of Congress Control Number: 2015909319

Print information available on the last page.

WestBow Press rev. date: 06/12/2015

Contents

Introduction

How many times have you looked at a sunset and thought of the peace and beauty of God? How often have you sat on a beach and thought of His never-ending love or the vastness of His power?

The world is full of things that can remind us of the character and attributes of our Heavenly Father and His love for us. It may be a tiny drop of water or a raging ocean…a baby's cry or the laughter of a child…a single blade of grass or a field of waving wheat.

The busyness of life can mask the little reminders of God as we struggle to keep up with our schedules of endless activities. We can look at a garden and only see the weeding that needs to be done, but miss the beauty of the blooming flowers. We can be in such a hurry to get to our next appointment that we overlook the hurting person right in front of us.

"Visions of Him" is a devotional book to remind you that God is in everything, if you will just take a moment to notice. Schedule time each day to read one of these devotionals and meditate on it. Open the pages of your Bible and discover for yourself what God's Word says. Underline or highlight the verses that touch you or speak to you. You may want to write notes in a journal each day. Make this a personal quiet time with Jesus as you read and then listen to what He brings to your mind and heart. At the end of each devotional, you will also find Scripture passages to help you dig a little deeper. God's Word is rich in truth and is a valuable guide for you each day. It is His gift to us.

This devotional book was written to remind us how important it is to look at the world around us and remember God's care, His love and His provision for each of us. Take time to notice "Visions of Him".

Grains of Sand

My family and I have spent countless hours on the long, beautiful stretches of beaches on the Oregon coast. There are strong, rugged rocks rising from the salty water, seagulls soaring overhead and miles of smooth, sandy beaches where people walk hand in hand. Dogs run freely and children dash about in the playful waves.

My favorite thing to do on the beach is to sit, pray, and sing worship songs as I contemplate the vastness of God. I pick up handfuls of sand and let the grains fall between my fingers. Occasionally, the greatness of the Lord overwhelms me and my tears, as salty as the ocean waves, fill my eyes and run down my cheeks. "Oh, Lord, how great Thou art! I am humbled in Your presence."

If you pick up one grain of sand, it is almost invisible in your hand; but if you pick up a handful, you see the different colors of crushed rocks and shells. Like a grain of sand, you may seem so small in a world of billions, but God cares about you and loves you with all His heart. He cares about where you have come from, how you got where you are today, and where you are going. He cares about your joys and sorrows, accomplishments and mistakes; but most of all, He cares about your relationship with Him.

Read Genesis 22:15-18 – Abraham was willing to sacrifice his son, Isaac; but God spared Isaac and blessed Abraham. God promised Abraham that He would make his descendents as numerous as the stars in the sky and as the sand on the seashore. Doesn't it make you smile to know that you are a descendent of a faithful man of God like Abraham? That the Almighty God loves you and values you as much as He does Abraham or anyone else on the planet? That each of us is like a grain of sand on a long stretch of beach, and collectively we make up generations of humanity whom God sacrificed His Son for? God blessed Abraham because of his obedience and He will do the same for us.

Visions of Him– The next time you are at the beach, take a moment to pick up one grain of sand and remember how much God values you. After that, pick up a handful of sand and realize that you are part of the family of God and think about what that means to you. We all have a place in His family.

Deeper Visions of Him – Read I Corinthians 12:12-27

The Royal Treatment

Have you ever wondered what it would be like to sit down with the queen of England and have a lovely chat? How about going out to dinner with a well-known sports figure, recording artist, or the president of the United States? Think about that for a moment. How would you prepare? What would you wear? Would you practice your handshake or curtsy? Would you mull over what you would say and maybe write down the questions you would like to ask?

One night, I was having a difficult time sleeping, so to keep from continuing to disturb my husband's rest, I went out to the living room, turned the television on and began to channel-surf. On C-span, Queen Elizabeth was addressing the British parliament in all the tradition of English royalty. She spoke quietly and carefully and her subjects listened with intensity and respect. Her husband, the duke of Edinburgh, was seated at her side and her ladies-in-waiting were standing nearby to attend to her every wish. When she completed her address, she rose from her gilded seat. Her subjects stood and remained standing as Her Highness and the duke made their way from the chambers to their horse-drawn carriage outside. It was truly a royal occasion.

Isn't it amazing that there is so much awe and respect shown for a human ruler, one with flaws like her own subjects? She rules supreme over a country as do many other presidents, kings, shahs and emperors. The Almighty God, the King of kings, created all these leaders, and we will stand alongside them before the throne one day. We will all bow before Him, and those who have put their faith in Jesus Christ will spend eternity in the presence of our Lord. We are all heirs to the Throne and will receive all the benefits of being called His child. Hallelujah! Now, that will be a royal occasion! "I can only imagine"!

Read Romans 8:12-21 – Life may be difficult or excruciating at times on this earth, but our King is also our Father, our Friend and our Savior. We call Him Abba Father.

Visions of Him – The next time you read or see anything concerning human royalty, remember that the King of kings is your Father and you are welcome to talk with Him anytime, anywhere. When you sing worship, you are talking to Him. When you are praying, you are talking to Him. When you read His Word, He is talking to you. You are royalty because He calls you His child and you have complete access to His throne. Smile, Prince or Princess!

Deeper Visions of Him – Read I Timothy 6:17-19

Dummies 101

Have you ever wondered who makes all those store dummies with the removable arms, perfect figures and painted faces? How do you choose a profession like that? Playing with dolls?

When you look at these plastic forms, you will notice there are no flaws: the lips are perfect, fingers are long and slender, the waist is in perfect proportion to the hips and chest, and any fashionable outfit looks fabulous on it. I must say, however, that the feet always look a little weird to me.

These dummies always have a smile on their face, but show little, if any emotion. There is no story to tell about its life, unless you make one up about a person who started out as a scientist, but then, for some strange reason, decided to change careers to become a store mannequin.

These dummies can be symbols of the countless people on our planet who walk around day after day with no emotions; just merely surviving in a lost world. You can hide an unhappy childhood, bad life choices, the pain of divorce or death of a loved one, but you can't hide it from God Himself. He sees every little corner of our lives, every pain, every joy, every accomplishment, every failure, and yet loves us just like we are; flaws and all.

Read John 4:1-42 – Jesus met the woman at the well and through His conversation with her, she realized that He knew her well. Zaccheus is another example of how the public saw a person they despised, but Jesus knew him and valued him.

How many times have we looked at someone and decided that they were not worthy of our time or care? They may be greatly different from us, dress in an offensive way or speak inappropriately, but they have a heart and a soul and God loves them as much as He loves us. Do you see them through your own eyes or through spiritual eyes? Do you see the eternal value of connecting with them by a touch or a prayer, or do you just walk by them like you do the dummies in a store?

Visions of Him – The next time you walk by a store dummy, remember I Samuel 16:7 "But the Lord said to Samuel, 'Do not consider his (Eliab) appearance or his height, for I have rejected him. The Lord does not look at the things man looks at. *Man looks at the outward appearance, but the Lord looks at the heart.*"

Deeper Visions of Him – Read Matthew 7:1-5

Up, Up and Away

Do you remember that song by the Fifth Dimension, waaaaay back in the 60s, called "Up, Up and Away"? The lyrics talked about the freedom of soaring high in a beautiful hot air balloon.

I don't know about you, but I have always wanted to step into one of those little baskets, slowly rise toward the heavens, and view the world from hundreds of feet above. I almost experienced it at Jackson Hole, Wyoming, but the day we were to go up, there was too much smoke from forest fires, so we were unable to go for the ride. I was disappointed, but knew that God must have had a reason why I was not to go. Someday I hope to enjoy a flight on a bright-colored balloon and check this item off my "bucket list". By the way, my husband has NO interest in sharing this experience with his adventurous wife! He said he would wave from the ground.

Our lives can be like hot air balloons sometimes. We want to live in freedom, and yet there are things that keep us tied solidly to the ground. It may be a bad relationship, choices that hold us back, insecurity, unforgiveness, fear, pride, anger, shame, or any number of other struggles.

Sometimes we decide we are not going to let these struggles hold us back anymore. We try to push them out of our minds and memories and not deal with them. We "fire up" and try to rise toward freedom, but those ropes tightly hold us down. We may try counseling, go to church more regularly, or remove ourselves from a bad situation, but we have not done the very thing that can break those ties once and for all...we have not "done business" with the Lord. We may not have confessed our sins, accepted His forgiveness, forgiven ourselves or forgiven those who have wronged us. These are strong ties that can hold down the biggest of balloons!

Read John 8:31-36 – God's grace is sufficient and strong enough to cut those ties that the enemy has used to keep you from being free in the joy of the Lord.

Visions of Him – The next time you see a hot air balloon floating in the sky above you, stop to thank Him for His goodness, His grace and His love that lifts you up so you can fly in His freedom. Look at what may be holding you back from His freedom, and break those "ties" once and for all.

Deeper Visions of Him – Isaiah 40:28-31

Roaring Rapids

When our children were very young, we took them to a beautiful resort called Inn of the Seventh Mountain in Central Oregon. We met my parents there and Grandma took care of Scott and Tami while my husband, father and I went river rafting on the Deschutes River.

We met our guide, put on our life jackets, listened to the instructions, and got settled in the big yellow rubber raft. It was smaller than I thought it would be, and I became nervous when I saw the action of the water rushing over the rocks. I began to have doubts. I'm not going to lie. I began to have BIG doubts actually!

Our guide told us to sit on the sides of the raft no matter how rocky it got. If we fell into the middle of the raft while going over the rapids, we were to get right back up on the side and continue paddling. Are you kidding?! As soon as we hit the rapids, I took my place in the bottom of the raft and stayed there until the ride was smooth again! I had two small children only 1/2 hour away and I wasn't going to leave them without a mother! I decided that day that river rafting was not for Scott and Tami's mom. Now, roller coasters are a different story!

Fear is a powerful emotion and it can keep us from enjoying all God has planned for us. It can be the fear of rejection, fear of failing, fear of having someone find out who we "really" are, fear of letting someone down, losing our job, losing control, or countless other fears. What fears are gripping you today?

Read Psalm 56:3-4, 11-13 – Fear can cripple us and when we become anxious, fearful or worried, we are telling God that we don't trust Him and His love and care for us. We either trust Him with our life or we don't. Think about those areas that have you covered in fear. Release them one by one to the Lord. Let Him prove His care for you and experience a life of growing trust, faith and hope in Him.

Visions of Him– The next time you see a rushing river, think of the rough waves of life and how even then, you can trust in your Protector, your Comforter, and your Healer to ride you through to safety.

Deeper Visions of Him – Read Psalms 46

Walking Side By Side

Several years ago, I was driving in downtown Eugene and came to a stoplight. As I waited for the light to turn, I looked around to see my surroundings and I noticed several shops, a bank, and a restaurant or two. My attention was diverted to a middle-aged couple walking on the sidewalk. I noticed that the woman had a problem walking and had a significant limp, which caused her to have a difficult time maneuvering from curb to curb. Then I realized that her companion was walking beside her; not before her, not behind her, but matching her stride step by step. No wonder she was smiling so much as she walked with him.

This scene reminded me of how the Lord would have us walk with one another in love; step by step, mile by mile, and day by day. God didn't mean for us to live as an "island", but to live as a family; His family. Each one of us goes through countless challenges in our lives. There are times to *give* comfort and help and there are times to *receive* comfort and help. Sure, it is easier to give assistance than it is to receive. You know how good it feels and what a blessing it is to help someone, right? Well, why would you deny others the blessing of helping you when you are in need? We are a family and it might just be your turn to let the "family" bless you. During or after a crisis, friends may want to bring meals, or give financial help when your funds have been depleted. It may be time to let the Lord bless you with His provision through His family. When you are struggling with personal issues, there may be someone He puts in your life to encourage you. Don't let self-focused pride keep you from receiving His blessings and blessing the ones who are serving you. It's how His family works!

Read Ephesians 4:11-16 – By caring and loving one another in the family of God, we can experience how wide and long and deep the love of Christ

11

is. Caring and loving one another should be free flowing and led by the Holy Spirit. "They will know we are Christians by our love."

<u>Visions of Him</u> – The next time you find yourself in need, accept the blessing of someone's offer to help, realizing it is God's provision for you through the body of Christ. His love and care for us is limitless, so let's not put our own limits on it!

<u>Deeper Visions of Him</u> – ("One another" verses) Romans 12:10, 16; Romans 15:7; 1 Corinthians 16:20; Ephesians 4:2; Colossians 3:13

The Final Score

"Five...four...three...two...one...GAME'S OVER! And the crowd goes wild!" Sports events can bring an extreme amount of enthusiasm, the pleasure of watching athletes give their all, and enjoying extraordinary competition. At the final buzzer, the winning team members throw their arms in the air, congratulate each other, and accept the admiration of the fans. On the other bench, however, deflated athletes sit and contemplate why their team was not victorious.

Are you a competitive person? Do you love to win? Will you do anything to beat someone or another team? On the other hand, how does it make you feel when you lose? Losing is never fun, but what is your reaction? Are you a gracious winner? Are you a poor loser?

America makes an art out of competition. We compete in sports, business, music, theatre, and products. We compete for jobs, recognition, relationships, and in just about every area of our lives. We compete in how our children do in school, how we dress, who has the best car, the prettiest yard and even whose house has the best Christmas lighting display.

Why is it so important to win? For every winner, there is a loser. Sometimes winning becomes too important in our marriages, friendships, and even in ministry. In a confrontation, if we are trying so hard to win, we are purposely trying to make our spouse, friend or colleague the loser. How does that translate into unity of marriage, unity of purpose, and success? I believe there is no room for that type of competition in healthy relationships. Think about it.

The Lord doesn't care who wins; He cares about our humility and faithfulness. He doesn't care how important we are on earth; He cares that we find our value and significance in Him. When we go to be with the Lord in Heaven, our goal should be to hear Him say, "Well done, my good and faithful servant." Not "You did better than so and so." Now, *that's* the final score!

Read Philippians 2:14-16 – Paul tells the church of Philippi that he wants to run with purpose and in doing so, shine for Christ in a spiritually dry world. What do people see in you? Do they see someone who shines brightly, someone who perseveres and runs the race with the strength of God? Get ready…get set…GO CHRISTIAN!

Visions of Him – The next time you watch a game, remember that we are victors because He is our Coach, our Guide, and our Prize for walking faithfully with Him.

Deeper Visions of Him– Hebrews 12:1-3

Sailing Toward the Sunset

One of the best things about living close to the Oregon coast is the opportunity in the evenings to watch the spectacular sunsets that paint the sky. The ever-changing colors mixing with the clouds treat sunset seekers to the work of the ultimate Artist. I am not an artist of paints, crafts or the like. I have other talents I use for the Lord. There have been countless times I have seen a sunset or a beautiful view that I wish I could recreate on canvas, but I will save that for Him and those He has gifted in that way.

Whenever I see a sunset, it reminds me that another day has ended and begins in another place around the world. The same sun we just saw go down behind the horizon in hues of pink, orange and red, will come up in Asia and their day will soon begin.

When I was a little girl, I remember my father saying, "When you lay your head on your pillow each night, ask yourself what you have done that has eternal value today." I remember that each evening when I see the sun set. "What have I done that has made a difference in someone's life? How have I represented the Lord today?"

Each day begins with new hopes, dreams, plans, and goals, and each day ends with memories, accomplishments, and hopes for a new day. Maybe our day ends with regrets of what could have been, but wasn't. Maybe we don't see hope for the future. God is there and He sees you, knows you, forgives you, and loves you unconditionally. You can have hope in Him when you can't have hope in your own efforts.

Read Psalm 4 – David is going back and forth as he calls out to God. He is struggling throughout the day, but he knows that he must look to God for His strength and joy. Look at verse 8. He knows that God is there by day and that His peace is firmly planted in him when he sleeps.

<u>Visions of Him</u> – The next time you see a beautiful sunset, ask yourself what you have done that day that had "eternal value." Who did God put in front of you and were you faithful in sharing His love and compassion with them? Don't waste a day!

<u>Deeper Visions of Him</u> – Read Ephesians 5 to see how we should live each day. Verses 1 and 2 give us the overall standard of how we are to imitate the Lord. How would that make a difference in our lives?

Snip and Pull

Saturday mornings always seemed to be the family "chore day" when we were kids. Every Saturday morning, after breakfast, Mom would begin her orders for the day. The bathrooms needed to be cleaned, the carpets needed to be vacuumed, the furniture needed to be dusted and then…there was yard work. Yuck! I have never enjoyed getting on my knees, digging in dirt, touching worms and avoiding bugs. I know there are millions of people on this earth who look forward to this activity, but I am not one of them.

On the days that yard work was on my chore list, I would drag my feet until I was reminded several times to get to work in the flower beds. Weeding seemed like a big waste of time because the weeds would be right back the next Saturday like clockwork. Many times, I would imagine a yard of pebbles and no weeds. Ahhhh! After weeding for 15 minutes or so, I would lie down on the grass, which someone would have just mowed, look up at the fluffy clouds and imagine what it would be like to fly. I would also make shapes out of the clouds and let my mind wander until I heard that familiar voice of my mother, "Robyn, are you finished weeding?"

I have often thought about how the Lord does weeding in us. Through His Holy Spirit, He finds those sins in us that keep us from holiness, exposes them and pulls them out. Sometimes we fight to keep the roots intact and live in our sin. Other times, we are sensitive to His leading, confess, and are freed from the bondage of our sin. Just like weed spray, which helps prevent weeds from growing again, the Word of God and our walk with Him can keep our sins from growing and taking over. Are there more weeds than there are flowers in your spiritual flower bed today?

Read 1 John 3:4-10 – Isn't it great to know that because God loves us so intensely, His Son paid the ultimate price for our sins? The weeds of sin will still pop up in our lives on a daily basis, but our choices and efforts to live a Godly walk can keep them down to a minimum, and then our relationship with our Gardener can choke the "weeds" out.

Visions of Him – The next time you spend time weeding a flower bed, remember with each weed pulled, God's amazing forgiveness is for you. He not only forgives; He forgets, just like you forget about the weeds once you throw them away. Strive for holiness and a life blooming for Him.

Deeper Visions of Him – Psalms 51:1-12

Christmas Impressions

I love decorating our beautiful Christmas tree for the holiday season. Before I developed allergies, we would search high and low for the perfect grand fir; a perfect cone shape with the perfect branch at the top to hold our perfect angel. We would decorate the tree with my mother's crystal ornaments and hundreds of twinkly white lights.

One particular year, the activities of the season seemed to overtake us and we ended up going to a local home improvement store where we settled for a premium Douglas fir, which cost us only $10. That price will speak to my accountant husband's heart every time! We threw the tree in the back of our SUV and hurriedly brought it into the house, got it in the tree stand, lightly flocked it and let it sit for a couple of hours. Now the time came to pull the ornament boxes out and trim our cheap tree.

As I began to put those precious ornaments on each branch, I realized that it didn't matter what the cost of the tree was. The beauty came from the sentimental treasures I placed on it. The weaker branches of this type of tree seemed to disappear between the sparkly crystal stars, cones and twinkly bulbs. When we finished decorating our tree by placing the angel on the top, we stood back and admired the beauty of our find. It would bring us many hours of pleasure throughout the rest of the holidays. We were grateful for what we saw before us.

This less-than-perfect tree reminded me of how imperfect we are as human beings. We have many flaws, some that show and some that do not. We try to hide those things that would cause others to think less of us. Just like the ornaments and lights on a Christmas tree, when we decorate ourselves with the character of God, it will take the attention away from the flaws and impurities in our life. When we place His grace, mercy, faithfulness, forgiveness, unconditional love and His joy in every area of our life, those around us will see *Him* more than they see us. As the verse in John 3:30 says, "I must decrease so He can increase."

Read Galatians 5:22-26 – When you look at the different elements of the fruit of the Spirit in this passage, take a moment to inventory the "ornaments" of your life.

Visions of Him – Next Christmas, when you are admiring your tree, consider how many ornaments of God are decorating your life. What do others see of God in you?

Deeper Visions of Him – Luke 8: 16-18

Show Me a Sign

Signs, signs, signs…They are everywhere! One evening, I was sitting in the car while my husband was buying milk. As I waited, I noticed that signs were covering the store windows, almost to the point of me being unable to see inside the store.

There were signs that prohibited smoking, prohibited us from walking in without shirts or shoes, advised us that the clerks didn't have large bills in cash, that no alcohol would be given to minors, there were no public restrooms available, etc., etc. I was amazed how many rules and regulations were plastered along the windows with endless ads.

There are countless street signs, billboards, and reader boards advertising goods and services, guiding us, and telling us what to do or not to do. It is a wonder we can think for ourselves, isn't it? There are detour, one way, speed limit, and turn only signs. There are u-turn signs, no trespassing signs, do not park signs, walk and do not walk signs, and even signs that tell you who should go first. There can be consequences, good and bad, depending on if we see a sign and if we choose to honor it or not. If we don't follow the signs, we can get lost, get a ticket or even worse, get in an accident.

The Holy Spirit guides and directs us in many ways on a daily basis. We may be very sensitive to His leading or we may ignore Him. We also have the choice to follow that leading or take matters into our own hands. We will certainly face the consequences of our choices, good or bad. God's one way, no trespassing, walk, and stop signs are made with His faithful, never-ending love and direction in mind for us. He knows what is beyond the signs and He always has our best interest at heart.

Read Psalm 25:4-12 – If we ask the Lord to show us His path as David does in this psalm, we must be willing to submit to His guidance. We can follow Him with full assurance of His love for us because He is trustworthy, faithful, and He will lead us on the right road.

Visions of Him – Be aware of the signs around you today and think about what the Lord might be telling you. Where would He have you walk or not walk, stop or go, or not trespass or yield?

Deeper Visions of Him – Psalm 119:129-134

Company Is Coming!

Your guests are due to arrive in half an hour! Are you feverishly picking up your children's toys, wiping the faucets in the restrooms, or making the last bed before heading to the shower and getting dressed in something nice?

Whenever I am expecting guests, I want to make sure that our home and yard are presentable. I am very fond of crystal stemware, platters and plates and I try to use them whenever I can. I enjoy honoring people and letting them know they are worthy of a little "pampering".

Not long ago, I realized that I worked hard at cleaning only the areas where our company would be and leaving the other rooms of the house in somewhat of a messy state. Our front yard was in great condition while our back yard was pretty much ignored. I realized that there was an element of hypocrisy in all of this.

It reminds me of the many times I have heard talk about the hypocrisy of Christians; how we act one way at church and then live an entirely different life during the week. We put on a smiley, perfect face and then when our Christian friends are not looking, we walk a life of gossip, profanity, judgment, criticism, and sinful ways. We walk into the church looking all put together, and the minute we get in the car, we begin to scream at each other. When we get home from church, we place our Bible on the shelf where it stays until the next Sunday. We talk about how important it is to spend time in the Word and in prayer, but barely remember to thank the Lord for the food at the table, let alone open the Bible or spend time in focused prayer.

Just like the perfect front yard and the disastrous back yard, or the immaculate front room and the chaotic back room, our lives have different areas that need to be exposed so the Holy Spirit can illuminate them.

When we let Him enlighten our "corners", we can begin to clean "the whole house" and enjoy more freedom in Him.

Read 1 Chronicles 28:9-10 - It can be easy to fool human beings, but how does it make you feel knowing that God sees you and understands every motive behind every one of your thoughts and actions? Does that make you nervous or does it give you comfort?

Visions of Him – The next time company is coming and you are cleaning the house, remember how the Holy Spirit is waiting to illuminate the areas of your life that need His healing touch. His "cleaning supplies" include love, forgiveness, grace, compassion, freedom and mercy.

Deeper Visions of Him – Psalm 139:23-24

Getting Off the Hook

One of the activities my husband, Ivan, and I like to do is to go fishing. We live within ½ hour of about 5 beautiful lakes and all of them are full of thousands of tasty trout along with bass, bluegill, and perch. I have to admit that I am a sissy fisherwoman at best. Ivan carefully threads the rod with the line. Since I am not inclined to touch the worm, he puts it and the corn on the hook and sprays it with his secret weapon, WD 40, which "is an attractant", he says. He then hands the prepared rod to me and I throw it in the water to wait for a strike.

It usually isn't long before I feel that familiar tug on my line. I reel in my catch and let Ivan take the fish off the hook and throw it in the bucket. I can only imagine what you are thinking. "That's not fishing; that's just pretending to fish!" Oh, I am sure you already have figured out that Ivan cleans the fish too, right? My responsibilities for fishing/camping trips in the past were to plan, buy and prepare the food, pack the bags, pack the car, set up the tent and make a "camping home" when we arrived. We were completely content with this way of doing things together. It worked for us. These days, it's all about renting a nice cabin and walking to the docks.

I have often thought about the concept of forgiveness. I heard one woman say, "Forgiving someone is not letting *them* off the hook, but taking *yourself* off the hook". I think it is both. When others hurt us, we have been hooked and it can be horribly painful. To even think about forgiving them can seem completely out of the question. We may say, "Why would I give them the satisfaction of my forgiving them? They don't deserve it one bit. I am never going to talk to them again!"

Forgiveness is a matter of obedience to the Lord, since He tells us to forgive those who have offended us. This doesn't mean we have to be best friends with them or even associate with them, but we must release them and the bondage unforgiveness has over us. Do you see that not forgiving and staying angry and bitter means that they still have a great amount of power over you? *You* are letting them keep *you* from joy and freedom, which keeps *you* from truly moving forward to be the best *you* can be.

Read Colossians 3:12-14 – Look especially at vs. 13. Just think of the endless times the Lord has forgiven us for the sins we commit each day. He is faithful to forgive (I John 1:9) every one of us on a daily basis, and it is important for us to follow His example by taking ourselves "off the hook of unforgiveness."

Visions of Him – The next time you go fishing, contemplate if there is someone who you need to forgive, so both of you can get off the hook and move on. Forgiveness is a matter of obedience to God and He deserves our submission and faithfulness to Him. Think of the offense and the offender and say, *"I RELEASE YOU FROM THE PAIN YOU CAUSED ME. IT WILL HAVE NO POWER OVER ME…ANYMORE!"*

Deeper Visions of Him – Matthew 6:14-15; Luke 6:37, 38

Lifelong Gifts

When I was in high school, there was a woman in our church named Mrs. Wells, who had the most amazing way of using her spiritual gift of encouragement. Directly after I graduated from high school, she generously paid my way to Europe to be part of a singing group for six weeks. I sang at her late husband's funeral and she said, "Oh, Honey, Charlie would have loved for me to do this for you! Jesus loves you and has big plans for you." I couldn't believe her generosity! Through the next few years, she never missed a chance to encourage me by saying things like, 'Oh, Honey, Jesus loves you so much" and "Jesus just shines through you and He has big plans for you."

I remember the day my family took her to a nursing home. She was a frail woman and didn't have much longer to live. As I stood by her bed, she motioned for me to bend down so she could whisper something to me. In her quiet, sweet, and weak little voice, she said, "Oh, Honey, Jesus loves you so much. You keep serving Him every day. He has big plans for you." I still weep when I remember her and the love she showed me. What I learned that day is that Mrs. Wells was using her spiritual gift of encouragement until the day she went to be with Jesus. I vowed that day to dedicate my gifts and talents to Him for the rest of my life. I would use them for no other purpose. I have kept that vow to this day.

God has gifted you in many ways. You may have the gift of encouragement like Mrs. Wells, or maybe mercy, compassion, exhortation, leadership, teaching or any number of others. You may not even know which gifts you have. You can find studies about spiritual gifts at the Christian bookstore or online that can help you recognize them and use them for God's purpose in you. Discover the gifts He has given you. Open them and use them liberally with the guidance of the Holy Spirit. Use them until the day you go to be with the Lord, just like Mrs. Wells.

Read Romans 12:3-8 – Spiritual gifts are not something that we use to glorify ourselves, but to bring glory and honor to God. They are for His use and purposes, and the blessing for us is that we can be used of Him in meaningful ways.

Visions of Him – The next time you open a gift someone has given you, think about the spiritual gifts the Lord has provided for His purposes. "Oh, Honey, Jesus loves you and has big plans for you."

Deeper Visions of Him – 1 Corinthians 12:1-11

New Glasses

I have worn glasses since I was eight years old. At that time, our family lived in Alaska when I was in elementary school. One Christmas our neighbor, Miss Collins, asked me to come to her house and help her string cranberries for her Christmas tree.

She gave me a needle, a strand of thread, along with a bowl full of plump, red cranberries, and set me to work. I had great difficulty threading the needle. I squinted, held the needle at different angles and even licked the end of the thread until it went limp. Miss Collins noticed me struggling at her dining table and came over to assist me. When we walked back to my house that evening, she told my mother about the difficulty I had and suggested that I be taken to the eye doctor. It wasn't long before I began wearing glasses.

There are different types of glasses. There are sunglasses, rose-colored glasses, bifocals, trifocals, reading glasses, safety glasses, and so many more. Although better eyesight is the goal, each type of eyewear has its own purpose and its own style.

Spiritual sunglasses hide the harsh sunlight and sometimes, because of the way we live, we can't handle the True Light for very long. Our *spiritual rose-colored glasses* can cause us to see the world unrealistically, so we don't see the needs of people or how we can minister to others. *Spiritual bifocals* can help us see the big picture as well as magnify the things the Holy Spirit is trying to draw our attention to. *Spiritual trifocals* can help us see close up and personal, the big picture and also the things of God. Each of us sees the Lord in different ways and we also see the world around us in different ways, depending on our experiences.

Whatever type of spiritual glasses we wear, our goal should be to see the Lord clearly. Many things in this world can cloud our vision of Him, so keeping our glasses clean and well-adjusted will make it easier to see. The best way to do that is to dig into God's Word, and really see who He is and what He is saying. Then receive it so that you can apply what you have learned with a clearer vision.

Read Proverbs 4:25-27 – A joyous life is one where our spiritual eyes are clear and with the Holy Spirit's guidance, we can see the path ahead. Spend some time in prayer and ask the Lord to remove distortions from the enemy so you can see Him clearly.

Visions of Him– The next time you put on a pair of glasses, whatever type they may be, remember that God has provided His Word to look at, to study, to examine, and through His Holy Spirit, to see His plan for you. Your goal? 20/20 vision, of course!

Deeper Visions of Him – Psalm 119:30-37

Sharpening the Blades

Several years ago, our community was hit by a windstorm like no other. I was in my office at Camp Harlow and saw the trees bending in the fierce wind gusts. Branches were flying by my window along with other pieces of debris. I opened my door that led outside and watched a fairly large fir tree slowly lay down across the lawn, eventually exposing its roots.

The electricity went out and employees began to scurry around trying to secure doors and assess the damage. One of the trees began leaning on an electrical cable and the pole itself began to lean. That was when we were told to leave the property immediately. Those were tense moments, to say the least!

The next day, we came back to work to see what damage this fierce wind storm had done. We lost 23 trees that day and the entire campground was covered in debris. It didn't take long for groups of men to arrive with gas-powered saws to cut the fallen trees into removable-sized pieces to sell as firewood. For a couple of days, each moment was filled with the sound of whirring saws and men's voices as they went about their work. People from our church came out to help and it made camp a very busy place indeed.

There were a few times we noticed that it became unusually quiet, and we assumed that the men were taking a break from their hard work. When we walked out onto the grounds, what we found was that the men were sitting on big cut logs and sharpening the blades of their saws so they could do their work more efficiently.

Dave, my former boss, noticed their activity and talked about how this related to serving in our camp ministry. We worked tirelessly, day after day, trying to attend to every detail of camp. There was an enormous amount of demand on us and we struggled sometimes to keep up. We prayed and asked for strength and guidance, but we didn't often take time to "sharpen the blades". God's Word and concentrated time in prayer were the best tools to "sharpen the blades" of our walk with Him. Others may have thought we were not getting things done when we were sitting and reading His Word, but that time was invaluable to the tasks before us. It was the groundwork of our labor.

Read Colossians 3:15-17 – We can read the Bible all day, but if we do not apply it, what's the use? We must pursue God through reading His Word, memorizing and meditating on it, and then absorbing and applying His truths into our life. Take the time each day to "sharpen your blades" so you can experience a more precise walk with God.

Visions of Him – The next time you hear a gas-powered saw whirring at its task, ask yourself, "When was the last time I "sharpened my spiritual blades"?

"Deeper Visions of Him – Read Hebrews 4:12-13

And the Wheels Go Round and Round

Do you remember the first time you were able to ride a bicycle without any help? Your mom or dad spent many hours holding onto the handlebars and/or the back of the seat while you carefully pedaled and hoped not to fall again. Then the time came when your parent said, "I think you've got it. Why don't you try to ride all by yourself?"

I remember my little red two-wheeler bike and how proud I was when I first decided to ride away from my dad all by myself. I nervously gripped the handlebars, put my right foot on the pedal, pushed forward and lifted my other foot to the pedal. Within seconds, the front wheel was wobbling side to side, my feet came off the pedals and I found myself lying face down on the sidewalk. My dad came running over, lifted me into his arms, wiped my tears and said, "Let's try it again." After some hesitation, I agreed and got back on that red bike with my dirty little face streaked with tears. After six or seven times of failed attempts, I began to get the hang of it and it wasn't long before I took off down the sidewalk full of pride at my new accomplishment. I couldn't wait to show my mom and my siblings! My dad took me in his arms again and this time, and he said, "Good job, Honey. I am so proud of you. You didn't give up."

How many times have you tried to accomplish a task or a skill and failed? How many times did you feel like giving up, because it was too hard or the task took too long to complete? Now think of times that you persevered, pressed on, and finally completed a task or met a goal? It could have been a goal such as losing weight, cleaning a room in your home, landscaping a yard, running a marathon, giving a report at school or work, or giving a speech. Didn't you feel exhilarated and glad you kept going until you finished?

The Lord wants you to succeed in all that He has for you to do. My dad always said, "If God has called you to do something, it means He has equipped you and He goes before you. If you have done your very best to prepare for the task, trust Him and then get out there and let Him do His business through you." Your "Father knows best."

Read James 1:12 – What trials are you facing today that are holding you back from accomplishing what the Lord would have you do? Persevere through each setback, and continue to ask God for His direction and strength. Take another step forward, and pretty soon you'll be "riding your bike" with confidence and success.

Visions of Him – The next time you feel like giving up or don't have the confidence to move toward a goal, remember that it is just like learning to ride the bike for the first time. You must keep trying until you succeed. You have a Heavenly Father who is saying, "Let's try again."

Deeper Visions of Him – 1 Peter 5:8-10

One of a Kind

When I was a little girl, we lived in the beautiful state of Alaska where my father pastored a church. For the first few years, we lived in an apartment in the back of Lake Spenard Baptist Church. It certainly was a short walk to church each Sunday!

The winter months were spent in darkness most of the years we were in Anchorage, because there were only 2 or 3 hours of daylight. It was during the short window of light when my sisters, brother and I would run outside to play in the snow. One particular year, there was a ten foot snowdrift against our fence which made the perfect sledding hill. Sometimes, I would sit in the fluffy snow and try to pick up one snowflake at a time and then blow it off my mitten. I felt like I was in a fairy wonderland and I was the princess. Not one of those delicate snowflakes was the same as another, but each one was as beautiful as the next.

That is how our Lord sees each of His children. We are all unique. He has given each of us unique talents, and has a perfect plan just for us. He knows our weaknesses and strengths. He knows every thought, every motive and every word we have ever said or will say. Every sin we have committed in the past, and will commit today or in the future, is already known by Him, yet He still loves us just the same as the rest of His children.

I have always struggled with the subject of racial prejudice, because in the Lord's eyes, we are all the same. He doesn't look at one of His black children any differently than he does at one of His white children or Indian children. It is sin in each of us who thinks our race is superior over the others. Oh, how He must grieve over disunity in His family!

He doesn't expect me to be a genius like those who are gifted in numbers like my husband, a gifted teacher like our pastor, or gifted in arts and crafts like my sister. God expects me to be the unique woman He made me to be. He expects me to accept myself for who He made me to be; not better or worse than anyone else. He wants me to be the best I can be, serve Him boldly and give Him the glory for it all. He expects the same of you.

Read Psalm 139 – What a truly remarkable thing to realize that your heavenly Father made you, knows you, treasures you and loves you just because you are you! No matter what another human being has told you, this is God's truth. Read this passage again and absorb the beautiful truth of it.

Visions of Him – The next time you are in the snow, pick up a handful, blow it off your glove and rejoice in the knowledge that God has made each of us to live as His unique creation and to cover the world with His love.

Deeper Visions of Him – Psalm 103:1-5

Ice Milk and Plastic Flowers

Have you ever tasted ice milk when you were expecting the decadent creaminess of rich ice cream? What a shock when you feel the crunchy little crystals instead of the smooth texture you were looking forward to. You can tell immediately that something is not right.

Think for a moment what it would be like to plant flower seeds in the spring and when they bloomed, they turned out to be plastic flowers. What?! How did this happen? I planted real seeds and they came up fake?!

Many things in life are imitation. Some are easy to detect and some look close to the real thing until you take a second look. There is fake hair color, fake diamonds, people who make a living being impersonators, imitation fruit drinks, fake sugar and even fake rocks. During this time, we can look at our TV screens and see stars who have had endless plastic surgery and "enhancements" that make them look more like plastic people. How sad to feel you need to alter so much to feel good about yourself or feel you are accepted. Sometimes you just have to ask, "What is real and what is not?"

What does a "real Christian" look like? Is it easy for people to know that Jesus is your Lord? Do your words tell them? Do your actions tell them? How about your integrity? Does your marriage represent Him well? Would others be surprised to hear that you are a child of God? These are hard questions for anyone, but important ones to ask if we are to determine if we are Christian impersonators or the genuine articles.

Read Ephesians 5:1-2 – In this passage, Paul exhorts us to be imitators of God. What would that look like if we imitated God in every way? How would our speech, our actions, activities or relationships be altered?

Beginning today, think about what areas of your life need to be a better imitation of God.

Visions of Him– The next time you find something that is imitation or fake, ask yourself if you are living life as an "imitator of Christ" or as an imposter.

Deeper Visions of Him – Psalm 86:11-13

Turn Down the Volume

The other day, I was stopped at a traffic light with my radio on, listening to a gentle worship song that was soothing and thought provoking. All of a sudden, a car stopped beside me with the volume of their music cranked up to the point where my body actually felt the pounding rap beat. I could hear almost every lyric of their song, whether I wanted to or not. I quickly closed my window.

Several thoughts came to mind; some I wish to share and some I do not. I wondered if the teenager in that car would be able to hear a siren, if their hearing would be impaired soon, and how long it would be before they would blow out their speakers. The deep thumping bass of that car next to me had distorted my time of worship. When the light changed, I opened my window again and drove on.

There are very few places where we can find true peace in our world today; traffic, music, conversation, televisions blaring, phones ringing and endless noises coming from all directions. It seems like the only time we can get away from it is when we are sleeping, and sometimes, that is even restless.

Where do you go to get away from the chaotic world you live in? Is it to the mountains, the beach, a little nook in your home, a park or somewhere else? When is the last time you sat in complete silence, took a long, deep breath and let the peace of God surround you? Why don't you try it right now? Take a deep breath and slowly fill your lungs with air. Now gently and completely let that breath leave your body. Do that five to ten times and then ask the Lord to fill you with His peace today. Take time throughout the day to repeat these "peace pauses" and enjoy the peace of God. He can speak to us anytime and anywhere, but it is easier for us to hear with a quiet heart. Shhhhh.

Read Philippians 4:7-9 – Look at the list in verse 8 and evaluate what things you fill your mind with. Now think about how much of your life is peaceful. Ask the Lord to fill you with His peace, and then try to eliminate the things that may be fighting against it.

Visions of Him – The next time you are faced with an overwhelming amount of noise and chaos, stop for a "peace pause" and ask the Lord to fill you with His peace. And about that loud music…turn down the volume!

Deeper Visions of Him – 2 Timothy 2:22-26

Just a Minute

"I'll be there in just a minute." "Just a minute, Honey, and I will get you a glass of milk." "I'll be with you in just a minute, Ma'am." "I said, "*Just a minute!*" How many times have we heard these words in our lifetime? We ask for something or someone's attention, and we get put on the back burner until they have the time to address our desire or demand. It can be annoying, irritating, and patience can become impossible.

This scenario is sometimes played out in our prayer life, isn't it? We ask God for things, sometimes even using Him as a "heavenly candy store." "Lord, I'll have one of those and two of those and…" Sound familiar? I have found myself doing the same thing. I want it when I want it and expect the Lord to answer the way I think is the best. Sometimes I pray several times a day about something and get no answer and I feel like God is saying, "I'll be with you in just a minute." After all, the Word of God says, "Pray without ceasing", right? Then, why isn't He answering me now? Oh, how naïve and impatient we can be!

He is our Heavenly Father, our Protector, our Comforter and He knows all things. He knows what is best, when the timing is perfect and He asks us to trust Him for *all* things. He knows the plan He has for you and for me and He always wants the best for us. Our prayers should always include, "…if it is Your will…" A minute is nothing to Him, but can seem like a lifetime to us. The question is, "Do we trust Him with our life or not?"

Read Jeremiah 29:11-14a – We, as human beings, have such a small knowledge of our life, our future, and certainly God's plan for us. He knows when the time is best for that career move, when to buy that house, when to pursue a relationship, etc. Pursue Him and His timing for your decisions and your future. We know but a speck of the whole picture, but He knows every single speck of our entire life, knows what is best, and how they perfectly fit together. We don't have the right to demand or command the answer we want. We will not change the mind of the Almighty God. Don't step ahead of Him; follow Him. Trust!

<u>Visions of Him</u> – The next time you say "wait a minute" to someone, remember that He may ask the same of you when you pray. Trust Him for His perfect timing and wait a minute, an hour, a day, or for years for Him to answer the way He sees best.

<u>Deeper Visions of Him</u> – Psalm 25:1-15

This Too Shall Pass

My close friend, Dianne, went to have a mammogram and the doctor gave her the frightful news that she had a tumor in her right breast. It was devastating and seemed like a bad dream. Human emotions seemed to overtake her and her husband, Pat, and they needed some time to absorb the enormity of this news.

The doctor told them the procedures he would recommend, and Dianne and Pat considered the options. They decided on chemotherapy and some radiation to make sure the cancer would not return. As many of us know, chemotherapy is no picnic. One of the weirdest things is the certainty of losing all of your hair. The doctor told Dianne when that would happen, so she made plans with her daughter to go and pick out the wig that most resembled her natural tresses. It seemed surreal walking into that wig store and tears filled Dianne's eyes as she realized why she was there. When we talked about this experience, I remember telling her, "Dianne, this is just temporary. You only have four chemo treatments. Your hair will grow back. Please remember that."

God allows all kinds of challenges in our life to bring us closer to Him, to build our trust, and to show us His love in a deeper way. It may be the loss of a loved one, the loss of a job, an illness, or any number of struggles. These things will not last forever, even if they remain until He takes us home. Things can look enormous to us as human beings and fear can grip us, but the Lord is saying "Trust Me, I am with you every step of the way. This too shall pass."

Read Jeremiah 30:17 – This is the verse that the Lord gave to Dianne as she walked through this health crisis. Trust that He will also give you the strength you need in times of worry, struggles and crisis.

<u>Visions of Him</u> – The next time you wash your hair and notice a few strands on your hand, remember my friend, Dianne, and how her hair loss was temporary. Your struggles will be temporary and hopefully, you will have grown to be a stronger child of God because of them. Oh, by the way, I saw Dianne today and she is beginning to notice a little "peach fuzz" on her shiny head!

<u>Deeper Visions of Him</u> – Psalm 40:1-8

Living in a Cage

Every time I go to a zoo, my heart hurts a little bit for the animals that live in cages day after day, out of their natural environment. They can see what is outside of their cage, but it is impossible for them to break free and enjoy it. Can you imagine spending your life in the same square space 24/7 and never seeing anything outside of those limitations? My heart goes out to the animals in those situations. How difficult would it be for us if we were unable to get out and enjoy fresh air, go for a walk, see a movie, shop or even go to church?

This subject brought to mind the way we, as Christians, sometimes live. We are comfortable in our church buildings, only associating with other believers and surrounding ourselves exclusively with "Christian things." This is a safe place, right? We don't care to hear what unbelievers' opinions are on politics, religion or moral values. We know what we believe and what not to believe. It is easier for us to see others with differing views with a critical spirit. We may even demean them and feel superior rather than listening to them, trying to understand them, and seeing them through Jesus' eyes.

We are in this world to reach others for Christ and to show His love to those around us. We are to represent Him well and be an example of His saving grace. It is not our job to judge or change them; that is God's responsibility. We need to step out of our "Christian cages", step into the world and be the Lord's representatives. Join a club, take a class, join a gym or wherever your interest takes you, and make a point of meeting those who need to see the Lord in this world. There is a lot of hurt all around us and we can be a light of Jesus to them.

Read Matthew 5:13-16 – Jesus calls His children the salt and light of the world. Read this passage and try to envision each word picture and then think of yourself as each of these pictures.

Visions of Him – The next time you visit a zoo and walk past the endless cages of animals, remember that God doesn't want us to stay in our "Christian cages". He wants us to step out and bring His love to those in a lost world.

Deeper Visions of Him – 1 John 2:15-17

Waves of Life

On February 14, 2015, we celebrated our 41st wedding anniversary…Forty-one years of marriage to the same man. I could go on and on about my husband, Ivan, but I won't bore you with the endless accolades I would give him. A marriage beautifully thriving this long is an amazing blessing considering the society in which we live. As I write this, I am sitting in a hotel room on the sixth floor and watching the endless waves rise up and eventually lower to a smooth sandy beach on the Oregon coast.

Marriage is an interesting experience because it requires two individuals with their own backgrounds and issues, to come together and build a life as one unit. Easier said than done, right?

The rolling ocean waves remind me of the many waves of change there are in a marriage. At the beginning, are the hearts and flowers of romance, the excitement of physical intimacy, and the anticipation of every wave of life ahead. As waves of challenges build, things can get rocky and unsteady, sometimes to the extent of toppling small, unprepared vessels. If the vessel had been prepared and knew what to look for, chances are, it would not have sunk. In a marriage, we must be prepared for the struggles that surface, recognize them as an attack from the enemy, stand together against the ever-growing waves, and ride them out as one.

Watching the waves from my hotel window, I see that the large boisterous waves roll into small waves until they completely disappear onto the beach. A couple, who is dedicated to the Lord and to each other, will be able to grow from each challenge, forgive liberally, and love unconditionally. A marriage like that will be able to weather any storm, ride any wave, and last a lifetime.

Read Matthew 19:3-6 – This scripture is in the context of Pharisees asking Jesus about divorce, but the principle of two becoming one in marriage is clear.

Visions of Him – The next time you see the endless waves of a beautiful ocean, take a moment to ponder the challenges your marriage or your individual life has endured. If you have grown and matured, then the next challenge will appear like a smaller wave, and your vessel will be more secure.

Deeper Visions of Him - Ephesians 4:22-27

Resting in a Shady Spot

On a recent trip to Hawaii, my husband and I enjoyed a week of balmy breezes, the unexpected fragrance of gardenias, and the warmth of the tropical sun. We would spend hours snorkeling, sitting on the beach and lathering ourselves with sunscreen so we didn't look like crisp bacon. Most of the time, the temperature was perfect, around 80 degrees, but there were a few days when it crept up to almost 90. The increased heat made us think twice about spending endless hours in the sun, so we would seek out additional water to drink and find shade more often.

Since Hawaii is such a tourist Mecca, it was difficult to find shade under a beautiful palm tree. We had to get to the beach before 9:30 or 10:00 in the morning and set our blankets, coolers, and towels out to stake our area. Lugging our stuff from the car to our spot was usually a long, tedious walk as we tried to juggle all the supplies we would need for an enjoyable day at the beach. Once we got everything laid out and organized, we would flop down on our straw mats, grab a cold bottle of water, lay back, and enjoy the coolness of our shady tree.

This reminds me of people who walk into our churches every Sunday who have been burnt by unfortunate circumstances, bad choices, or just the general challenges of life. We walk in, all showered and nicely dressed, but inside, we may feel beat up, hassled, and undone by daily life. Just getting to the church can be a stressful experience! Sound familiar? We are all looking for a "shady spot" of soothing peace in our lives.

I have made it a Sunday morning habit to meet at least three new people each week. It is easy to talk with those we know. However, God calls us, as His family, to reach out in love and extend His arms to those who enter our church doors, as well as to those who are in our world during the week. We just might be the essential "shade" sad souls need as they enter our foyer on Sunday mornings. Try it!

Read Romans 12:9-13 – Showing the love of God is a ministry that can affect those to whom you demonstrate that love throughout their week.

Visions of Him - The next time you have an opportunity to sit in the cool shade of a tree, remember how God is your shade from the heat of your life. This Sunday, take the time to look around your church for someone who may need a kind word, a touch, or even just a smile. It may be the only "shade" they have felt in a long time.

Deeper Visions of Him – John 15:9-17

Reflections

When our children were infants, I remember having them look into a mirror and then watching their faces as they saw themselves changing their expressions, touching their cheek or puckering their lips. That one activity could keep their attention for a long time. The older they got, however, the more they seemed to look in the mirror, but in a different way. They would now notice the imperfections on their face or their bodies, and check out the outfit they put together for the day.

We all sneak glances at our reflections in windows, mirrors, or even in a smooth sheet of metal, don't we? It seems to be human nature to look at ourselves almost every chance we get. Sometimes we are pleased at what we see and sometimes we are not. Hello? Am I the only one?

The question is, "How do others see us?" Do they see the little imperfections, the blatant flaws, the issues that control us, or do they see the love and character of God? Do they see peace and contentment?

On a deeper level, how do we see ourselves? Do we see what Jesus Christ sees...a beloved child of His, someone who is precious in His sight, and has lots of potential, or do we see ourselves from a human point of view...someone who has endless flaws, a sinner without grace and a life of shame, hurt, guilt and unforgiveness?

Look in the mirror again and this time, remember that the face you see is one that the Almighty God sees and treasures. He loves the person in that reflection and no matter how that reflection ages and changes, He'll still love you just the same...with His complete and unconditional love.

Read James 1:22-25 – When you look in the mirror this morning, do you see a smile of the freedom and joy of God or a scowl of doubt and mistrust? Our expressions most times reflect what is within. Ask Him, at the beginning of this day, to give you peace and to soothe your soul with the knowledge that He is walking right in front of you with every step you take.

Visions of Him – The next time you look at your reflection, ask yourself how others may see you and remember that God sees you the clearest of all and still deeply loves you.

Deeper Visions of Him – 2 Corinthians 3:7-18

Looking For a Sale

The day after Thanksgiving has become almost as exciting as Thanksgiving Day itself to the women in our family. If you are a shopper, you will understand this and if you are not a shopper, you are probably rolling your eyes right now. You can't even think about the long lines, overflowing parking lots, a multitude of shopping bags and the constant flow of credit cards and hard cash!

Our Thanksgiving Day begins when we put the big stuffed turkey in the oven. Directly from there, our daughter, Tami and I walk out to the front porch to retrieve the five pound newspaper; three quarters of which are the ads for the next day's shopping marathon. We turn on the Macy's Thanksgiving Parade, sit on our bed, armed with pens and notepads, and sort through the ads to plan our day of shopping for this year's Christmas gifts. The next day is almost like another holiday in itself to these Besemann women!

I try to never buy things that are not on sale and our daughter is the same way. It seems pointless to spend more money than we need to. We take notes from the newspaper ads and compare prices until we find the best deals. Then we plan our itinerary to make the most of our time and gas mileage. It is an event!

This annual tradition reminds me of the way we, as Christians, try to cut our walk with God short to fit our own needs and comfort level. We may not want to make the *whole* commitment to Him. We may try to cut it 25% by maybe cheating on our tax return, or cut 50% off by living differently during the week than we do on Sunday. God asks that we pay full price, live a life worthy of our calling, and enjoy the quality of a life fully aligned with Him. Don't be one who looks for a spiritual bargain. Pay full price and enjoy the endless and eternal benefits.

Read 1 Chronicles 16:8-11; Proverbs 16:3 – Are you fully committed to God? Only you can answer that question. Actually, only you *and* God can answer that question.

Visions of Him – The next time you go shopping and see sale promotions, remember that paying full price spiritually is a lot better than looking for a spiritual sale to save you a percentage on your commitment to the Lord.

Deeper Visions of Him – Psalm 37:1-9

A Refreshing Fragrance

I used to work for a man who wore so much cologne/aftershave that we could smell him way before we saw him! The fragrance was not offensive, just obvious and long lasting, shall we say? Some of our church choir members have allergies to fragrances, so we have asked that fellow singers not wear perfume or aftershave because of the effect it has on others around them. Wow! What a contrast, huh?

There is an endless selection of perfumes, colognes, aftershaves and even "toilet water" that we can spray, splash, rub or dab on our skin. There are fruity, woodsy, flowery and exotic fragrances. There are bottles the size of a cotton ball all the way up to huge bottles that almost look like small vases and cost hundreds of dollars.

It is an interesting experience to step into a car with three other women, all wearing a different fragrance. Thank God for windows that open! Pretty soon you get used to the mixture and don't even notice it.

How many times have you been in a room when someone walks in who has an air of joy, confidence and pleasantness? Sometimes they say someone is a "breath of fresh air" or they just "light up a room". We, as believers, are told to be a fragrance of the Lord in our world. Our fragrance should be the very essence of the fruit of the Spirit. It should be full-strength, and not diluted in any way. That's the pure perfume of the Lord Jesus Christ, and not cheap cologne or toilet water.

Read 2 Corinthians 2:14-17 – The enemy of this world has filled it with the stench of anger, bitterness, violence, unforgiveness and darkness. We need to pour the fragrance of the Lord all over us from head to toe, inside and out and let the people around us "get a whiff" of Him.

<u>Visions of Him</u> – The next time you visit the perfume counter at the mall, take a good whiff of your favorite fragrance and remember that you are to be a pleasant fragrance of the Lord every day, no matter what the cost.

<u>Deeper Visions of Him</u> – Proverbs 16:7, 23-24

Slave or Servant

When I was a young student, long before computers, cell phones, or microwaves, I remember studying the servants in biblical times as well as the slaves in our own American history. Servants in the Bible were most often portrayed as willing people who usually had smiles on their faces while they served their masters. They were equated with us being servants of the Lord.

Slaves, in the south of our country, however, were forced to do their tasks under horrendous conditions much of the time. They were treated like animals, paid next to nothing for endless hours of back-breaking work and lived in dirty little shacks in the outlying areas of the land they worked. Even as a child, I was sensitive to the differences between these two types of service. I didn't understand how one human being could treat another so terribly as many masters did to slaves, since we are all equal in God's sight.

Do you view yourself as a slave or a servant of the Lord God? Do you serve Him with resentment or out of obligation? Do you willingly serve Him with a joyful heart and attention to the details of doing His will? Look deep.

God wants to be our Master, Leader and our Commander, but He does all of that with complete love for us and without an iron fist. He wants us to be all we can be and places us where we can succeed with His guidance. We need to strip away all the self-centered motives, the battle for our "rights", and surrender to a God Who is ready to lead us to freedom and victorious joy as we serve Him.

Read Galatians 4:1-7 – What an amazing truth that, as born again Christians, we are not only willing servants of our Heavenly Father, but we are His heirs as well! Now *that* is a worthy calling, isn't it?!

Visions of Him – Joshua 22:5; Ephesians 4:10-13 - God has put us on the earth to serve Him from a heart of love and devotion. One generation after another is called to serve Him out of love with all our hearts and souls. Are you giving Him your best or only the bare minimum?

Deeper Visions of Him– Luke 16:10-14

Building Bridges

Have you ever studied a bridge and wondered how they construct it so it stands strong for hundreds of years? How deep did divers have to go to get the foundations buried in the bottom of the ocean, sound, or river? How many tons of steel had to be used to insure that anyone passing over it would not fall into the depths of the water below?

There are steel bridges, some made of wood, and even small ones made of rope. Bridges can connect a mainland to an island, one state to another, and sometimes one country to the next. There are tall bridges, eight-lane bridges filled with rush hour traffic, famous bridges that are almost monuments, such as the Golden Gate Bridge, and some that are hidden deep inside forests that are precarious at best.

Many times, when we pass over a bridge, a spark of fear enters my mind, wondering what would happen if the bridge gave way. After all, if there is a collision, there is nowhere to go to avoid it. What if something on the bridge broke underneath and we were dumped into the churning water below? My mind can go crazy with worry, if I would let it!

Our connections with other people are like bridges. Some are fragile, some have strong foundations, some are narrow and some include many people, and are therefore wide. Through the years, we may have a damaged relationship, so the "bridge" needs to be repaired or even have an entire renovation. Both sides of the bridge need to be worked on, so there can be a repair of the bridge of friendship by meeting in the middle.

God asks us to "love one another", encourage one another, forgive one another and live in harmony. What "bridges" need some work done in your life? Is it a spouse, a family member, a co-worker, someone at church, or someone else? What are you willing to do to help repair the "bridges" in your life?

Read Matthew 5:9; Romans 12:16-21 – Take note of the words "anyone" and "everyone" in this passage. Who are the "anyones" and "everyones" in your life toward whom you need to build a stronger bridge?

Visions of Him – The next time you go over a bridge, think about the "bridges" in your life. Ask yourself which ones are weak and in need of repair and what you can do to fix your end of it. Which "bridges" are strong and steady? Keep them that way by doing your part.

Deeper Visions of Him – Titus 3:1-11

Where's the Remote?

What did we ever do before the invention of the TV remote control? Well, we had to get up every time we wanted to change the channel, adjust the volume or turn the set on or off. We would sit closer to the TV so we didn't have to walk so far.

In the twenty-first century, we have universal remotes that allow us to control stereos, dvd and cd players, video machines, window blinds, lights, and so much more. Every day brings more technology and more ways to allow us to stay on the couch or in the recliner.

Wouldn't it be great to have a remote to change the circumstances of our life and make it so we would not have to look at what annoys us? If we wanted to, we could just change the "channel" with the touch of a button or adjust the volume of someone talking to us. We would not have to face anything that we didn't want to; just see what's on the next station! We could avoid challenges in our marriage, our work situation, difficulties with our kids, and never have to look at them or work on them. What an easy way out of life, right?

God allows those challenges for a reason. He wants us to grow, to recognize His provision for us, to accept His lessons, and ultimately to experience a stronger trust in Him. These would all result in a more victorious and joyful life. If all we had to do was push a button to avoid those challenges, we would never grow or see Him at work in our lives. God has the perfect plan and knew what it was before we were even born. We are the ones who stray from that plan, but yet, He still continues to guide us back to Himself. Now, whether we will relinquish the remote control or not is our choice!

Read 2 Corinthians 12:9-10 – This scripture is a wonderful reminder that no matter how many challenges we face, we don't have to "change the channel", because His strength is sufficient.

Visions of Him – Take a moment to sit and hold your remote control and think about this. Look at the challenges that are presently in your life. Why do you think God has allowed them? Would it be better if you could use a remote control and avoid struggles altogether, or are you willing to set the remote aside and learn His lessons so you can become a stronger man or woman of God?

Deeper Visions of Him – Romans 5:1-5

Questions, Questions, Questions

What time is it? How are you? Are we there yet? Would you like fries with that? Are you serious? Why did you do that? Do you love me? Our days are filled with questions and for every question, there is an answer. There can be truthful answers or lies, straight-up answers, or beating-around-the-bush answers.

I remember when our children were in their pre-school years. It seemed like their inquiring little minds were on overload and never quit working. This was a big world they were living in and there was so much to learn. No matter how tired I was, it was important that I taught them as much as I could before they "left the nest"…for kindergarten.

How many times have we asked God questions like: "Why are you allowing this in my life?" "Do You hear me when I call out to You?" "Do You even see me?" Why did they have to die so young, Lord?" Can You forgive me one more time?" "Why didn't You answer my prayer?" "Are You alive and real?"

God hears every question, patiently answers in His timing, shows us His will, and waits to hear from our own inquiring minds. You see, God has the answer to every one of our struggles, our doubts, and our fears. He wants to hear that we even want His opinion, guidance and answers. God is all-knowing, has all the answers and is waiting for your endless questions right now. Ask away!

Read 1 John 3:19,20 – "He knows *everything*." This means there is not a question that you can ask Him that He won't have the answer to, so start asking! The bigger challenge, however, is waiting for Him to answer.

<u>Visions of Him</u> – Take a few minutes and on a sheet of paper, write down some of the questions you would ask God if you saw Him face to face. Pray over these questions and let Him show you His answers through His Word. Listen to what He lays on your mind and heart.

<u>Deeper Visions of Him</u> – Psalm 111:1-10

Fill 'Er Up

Can you believe the cost of gas nowadays?! I remember how outraged we were when we had to pay $1.00 per gallon! The price of gas always seemed to rise around Memorial Day and lower after Labor Day. Now we watch the price at the pumps fluctuate from day to day. It's like gas stations are in a perpetual gas war!

Do you remember when we could choose between regular and unleaded and now, regular *is* unleaded? These days, our choices of fuel are regular, plus, premium or diesel. Personally, we usually use regular, but will occasionally fill up with plus if we are going to be pulling the boat with our SUV and climb a mountain. It's nice to have the choice.

This reminds me of how we try to fill voids in our life with any number of things. We may be feeling lonely, isolated, or left out, and then we try to fill that void with another relationship, alcohol, drugs, meds, or activities. Filling ourselves up with these things can "fill our tank" for a little while, but are quickly emptied. Before long, the void returns and we find ourselves running on fumes again. Why?

Because, we are not filling ourselves up with the one Fuel that will keep us moving forward…Jesus Christ. He is completely available, costs only a willing heart, and will never run out of gas. Fill your spiritual tank with His Word, songs, and hymns. Go to His station in prayer, and then drive away full of all He has to offer you. His Fuel will make your journey richer, stronger and longer lasting than the inferior fuel the enemy has to offer.

Read Acts 2:25-28 – This passage reminds us that when we live according to God's riches, guidance and blessings, He will fill us with joy within His presence. It doesn't get any better than that, does it?

<u>Visions of Him</u> – The next time you are sitting at a gas station getting your tank filled, think about how you are filling your spiritual tank and what fuel you are putting in it. He is the Premium Fuel, so fill 'er up!

<u>Deeper Visions of Him</u> – Psalm 16:7-11

Terrible Twos

How many times have you been in a store and heard the familiar sound of a toddler having a screaming fit three aisles down? I almost immediately assume the child is about two years old and the mother is in a big power struggle with that "precious little treasure."

I remember when our daughter was two years old and had a fit in a store because she couldn't have a toy on the shelf. I immediately took her out to the car, talked with her, promptly spanked her and told her that every time...*every time* she had a fit, she would experience the same consequences. The next few times we arrived at the store and before we entered, I reminded her of that incident and what the consequences would be if she exercised her "tantrum muscles" again. I then spoke about positive things as we walked into the store. She never had another tantrum in a store again.

Spiritual tantrums before the Lord can be just as upsetting and damaging as a tantrum of a two year old child. We ask God for things to fill our desires, and for answers, but what we are really asking for is our own way. We, as human beings, are so short-sighted. We know what we want and expect God to answer our requests our way. We want *what* we want, *when* we want it, and *how* we want it. When we don't get it, we may ignore God by stopping our prayers to Him, not going to church, and step away from seeking Him through His Word. "After all, doesn't God care about me anymore? Doesn't He hear me anymore? Why do I bother asking Him for things anyway, if He isn't going to answer?" On and on and on...

Sometimes God has to "take us out to the car" and discipline us to bring us back in line with Him and His will. That can be painful, but needs to be done, so we are back in fellowship with Him and surrender our will to His. Doesn't it really come down to how much we trust Him with our life and His plan for us?

Read Jeremiah 29:11-14a – God knows the plans He has for us, which He knew before we were even born. He knows us inside and out and still loves us. Why do we think we know a better plan? He sees the whole picture of our lives and not just a humanly limited view.

Visions of Him – The next time you see or hear a two year old having a tantrum, remember, that as God's children, we need to live in obedience and not throw a fit every time He doesn't answer us the way we want Him to. He has our best interest at heart, Child. Time to grow up!

Deeper Visions of Him – Hebrews 12:1-13

Sheets, Blankets and Comforters

There has been a huge increase in what is available in stores and on television for home decorating. If we bought everything that is advertised, every corner of our home would be perfectly matched and could be featured in magazines and on decorating shows.

Bedding is one area that has exploded with options and ideas. Sheets come in muslin, satin, flannel, and everything from 150 thread count to over 500. There are even sheets made out of t-shirt material, for heaven's sake! Let's not even talk about the imbalance there is with the people of poor nations who sleep on dirt or straw mats or the homeless on our own streets and alleys! American excess again.

When I began to think about bedding, it reminded me of our lives and how we cover ourselves up personally and spiritually. Sheets are thin and come in all types of patterns, colors and materials. We begin to cover ourselves up when we are young. We don't want anyone to see some of the things we did and may feel shame about.

On top of our sheets, we usually place a blanket or two. Some are thick, some are thin, some are itchy, some are smooth, but all are meant to keep us warm. In our lives, we can cover ourselves to insulate us from the world and keep us in our comfort zone. People can't really see through our "personal blankets". We feel safe under them. Comforters have evolved into almost works of art and many times, sets include shams, pillows and bed skirts. No matter how wrinkled or messed up our sheets may be underneath, our comforters can hide the imperfections. You can't really see the blankets under the comforter, but you know they are there.

We can try to hide our guilt and shame under mountains of "bedding", but the Holy Spirit can see right through them, can peel the layers back, iron the wrinkles out, and help us enjoy a smoother life of forgiveness and grace. It will take time and can be a painful process, but oh, the comfort, peace, and joy we will experience will be well worth it!

Read Mark 4:21-25 – Believe that when you reveal yourself and stand open before the Lord God, He will bless you as He heals and forgives you for the things you have been covering up.

Visions of Him – The next time you make your bed, take your time with every layer. Ask the Lord to help you see the wrinkles of your life, and have Him pull the blankets back so you can live a life full of more joy and freedom.

Deeper Visions of Him – 2 Corinthians 4:1-2

Commercial Free

Do you ever get tired of those loud, crazy commercials on radio and television? Some of them are entertaining and can make you laugh and some are just plain annoying and can irritate you. Some are made to even make you cry.

When my husband and I record a show, we find it is always better to watch it later so we can skip those endless commercials. I wonder what the advertisers think of that. We sure aren't helping them make money, right? Now, I know hundreds of people, including advertising execs, actors, producers, and film editors who have worked countless hours to make these commercials. I also realize that companies pay millions of dollars to have their product promoted, but we live in America and we don't have to look at them if we choose not to.

Have you ever wished for a "commercial" in the challenges in your life? Wouldn't it be great to have a reprieve from the chaos and struggles? Maybe a commercial about something soothing, comforting or nurturing to take the stress away, if only for a few minutes.

If we think about it, we can sort of make our own "commercial breaks of life" by stopping to pray, thinking about the wonderful character of God, singing or listening to some worship songs, or even remembering a comforting scripture verse. We can turn our attention away from our pain or stress and then when our "commercial" is over, we can have a healthier and more peaceful perspective. Try it.

Read Colossians 1:10-14 – Life is a full-length feature, without commercial interruptions, so stand strong and see what personal and spiritual growth you will enjoy as the result of your perseverance.

<u>Visions of Him</u> – The next time a commercial comes on the radio or on the television, mute it, and take a moment to ask the Lord for peace through the challenges of your life or thank Him for His blessings. Breathe.

<u>Deeper Visions of Him</u>– Psalm 31:14-17, 23-24

Are You Talkin' To Me?

There have been many times when I have been between two people who are talking to me at the same time. My head moved from side to side as if I were an oscillating fan on high speed. I could pick up one word on my right and maybe two on my left. When both parties stopped talking, I would have comprehended virtually nothing and looked at each of them with a blank stare. Has that ever happened to you? If you are a parent of more than one child, I am sure it has!

This reminds me of when the Lord God tries to speak to us at the same time the enemy is trying to get our attention. This can happen in a store when the clerk has given us too much change, when someone at work gives us credit for something we didn't do, when we are attracted to someone other than our spouse, or any number of other scenarios where we have a decision to make between right or wrong.

Realizing that God is everywhere, knows everything, and uses the voice of His Holy Spirit in our lives, is an amazing resource when we come to these crossroads. At the same time, the enemy is standing by trying to influence us to ignore God's voice, turn away from Him, and step toward the wrong direction. Which voice are you going to listen to? Which voice is louder, and which direction will you go? God's way is right, truth and light; the enemy's way is destructive, misleading and hurtful. Stop turning your head from side to side. Only look to the "right" and accept God's leading.

Read Proverbs 16:1-7 – If we listen to God's voice over the evil one's voice, we will keep Satan's influence and temptations away and become more sensitive to the Holy Spirit's, thus winning the battle. Right now is the right time to listen to the right voice, amen? Listen.

Visions of Him— The next time you come to a crossroad of right or wrong, remember that God's way is *always* the best way. You don't have to have an oscillating conscience; just turn toward the "right" and walk in His direction.

Deeper Visions of Him – John 10:25-30

Whine or Worship

How many times have you been driving along the freeway and all of a sudden, you see the brake lights ahead of you light up, causing you to quickly apply your brakes? You then realize that there is a long line of cars ahead of you at a standstill and you once again see your busy schedule take a left turn. You may live in a big city where commutes seem endless day after day and tempers can flare with the stress of traffic jams, accidents or just the daily stream of automobiles on the roads.

There are choices at times like these…you can whine, complain, give other drivers a piece of your mind, bite your nails, talk on your cell phone by bluetooth, get progressively more irritated *or* you can turn the radio to a Christian station, put in a worship cd, or even listen to the Word of God on your mp3 player. What a perfect time to be alone with the Lord and spend those moments in His presence!

I don't live in a very big city, but when I visit one, I always have worship cds with me to make heavy traffic and freeway driving opportunities to commune with God and sit in His presence. Sometimes I get so involved in joyful worship, however, that my speed creeps up before I know it! I wonder if a traffic officer would understand my reasoning and let me off with a warning.

Fill the cd holder or mp3 player in your car with worship or music that brings you to a place of joy in the Lord. There are thousands of cds and downloads you can purchase on the internet or at your local Christian bookstore. Fill your car with the Lord and enjoy the ride. Watch your speed, though!

Read Psalm 28:7 – Lift up your voice in song and open your heart to freedom in praise. It will do your heart good and draw you closer to Jesus.

<u>Visions of Him</u> – The next time you find yourself in a big old traffic jam, take a deep breath and sing one of your favorite worship songs or hymns and remember that He is sitting right there in the car with you. Enjoy the ride!

<u>Deeper Visions of Him</u> – Psalm 104:33-34

Tape It Up

Have you ever said something you wished you hadn't and regretted it later? Would it have been better to tape your mouth shut so inappropriate or harmful words would not have escaped?

Well, I have a close friend who had been having some severe challenges with her husband. Even with the best intentions, she would let words escape that did more damage than good, which would then prolong the tension between them. One day, she decided that she needed to let the Holy Spirit speak to her husband without her opinions or interferences. Women are very good at letting their opinions be known and sometimes we just "want to help", but it doesn't help at all.

On one particular day, my friend decided that she needed to keep her opinions to herself, so when her husband headed toward an argument, she promptly walked to her desk, took some tape out of the drawer and placed two strips over her mouth for the next couple of hours. At first, he told her she was being very immature, but he soon realized that she meant business and her actions fizzled his attempts at confronting her. He was much more pleasant the rest of the day.

Our speech is to be flavored with love, encouragement, respect and words of God's wisdom. Words are powerful whether they are encouraging or discouraging, so we need to be aware whether it is time to "tape it up" or not.

Read Psalm 19:14 – Use this verse as a prayer as you ask for wisdom in what you say or don't say. Now, as situations come up, rely on the Holy Spirit's guidance and, if you need to, reach for "the invisible tape".

<u>Visions of Him</u> – The next time you use some tape on a gift or torn page, remember that a relationship can be protected or restored by figuratively placing tape over your mouth.

<u>Deeper Visions of Him</u> – Psalm 141

Righteous Recycling

Living in the beautiful state of Oregon for many years has been a delight and at the same time, "interesting". Oregonians are independent; taking pride in accepting diversity, voting for assisted suicide, fighting for gay rights for years, fighting for the spotted owl, and hugging trees. The majority of Oregonians tend to vote for liberal candidates and are known for leather sandals the size of snowshoes as well as brightly colored tie-dyed shirts, ties and even diapers. My husband struggles with all of this, however, it has been a great place to raise our children because it is a mid-sized town close to the mountains, lakes and the ocean. God has allowed us to build a great life here.

One of the important issues in our community is recycling. We recycle everything from plastic to glass to tires, to metal and paper. Large trucks come by once every other week and take our recycled items away to a huge center. I find it fascinating that even clothes can come from recycled items. How does that happen and where is it going to stop? Do my shoes come from a recycled rubber mat? Does my toothbrush come from an old plastic straw? Will my Bible come from a recycled adult magazine? Now, wouldn't *that* be an "interesting" thing?!

This past weekend, I watched as a young woman who had just suffered a miscarriage, minister to another young mom who had also suffered the same loss. As these two women were talking, I couldn't help but marvel at how the first woman was, in essence, recycling her pain so the other woman could use it for her own healing. Both women were in tears and had a deep connection as they spoke.

When we go through extreme struggles, many times we do not understand why God would allow this pain in our lives. We may question Him, doubt Him or just cry out to Him in agony. "Why, God, why?!"

We may never understand why, but what we can do, when the time is right, is minister to others who are suffering in the same way we have. We understand, we have felt that pain, so we can reach out and use our pain and what God has taught us for good. Don't let your hurt be for naught. Use your experiences to encourage and minister to others, so they can receive healing and strength from God through their crisis, just like you have. That's "righteous recycling"!

Read John 9:1-5 – The phrase, "but this happened so that the work of God might be displayed in this life", gives us a glimpse of why God allowed this man to be blind. How can you use a painful experience or circumstance in your life to bring someone closer to the Lord for comfort and healing?

Visions of Him – The next time you take the recycle bin out to the street or take those pop cans to the recycle center, remember that God doesn't allow a challenge to be just for you. You can "recycle" your experience and make something new out of it in someone else's life, if you are willing.

Deeper Visions of Him – Romans 9

Craft Crazy

Crafts seem to have taken over the world! There are silk flower crafts, pottery painting stores, scrap-booking parties and conventions, craft stores the size of roller rinks, and even classes on how to learn stained glass crafts. I will admit to you that I am indeed craft-impaired. There is no way that I can paint a recognizable flower on stemware or even make a bracelet out of beads that anyone would want to wear. I am just not gifted in this area. Now, I can do children's crafts all day long, such as coloring in color books, making a chocolate castle out of cookies and candy, or making an entire apartment out of play dough. I have done all of these with numerous children. Are you impressed?

My sister, Connie, on the other hand, is very artistic and creative and I have always been impressed with her ability to make something beautiful out of anything. She is so natural at it and she seems to always find new projects to exercise this talent. She is a hair stylist, cake decorator, painter, house decorator, and on and on.

This makes me think about the Lord and how He takes the experiences of our lives to creatively use them for our growth and for His glory. I went to a Christian aerobics class and eventually became the director of a large gospel aerobics program called Lord in Fun Exercise (L.I.F.E. in the '80s). Since I have always been a large person and was never allowed to dance in our family, this *was* really creative of the Lord. I choreographed hundreds of routines during the eight years I led that ministry. When I resigned as director, we had 50 instructors and 1500 students.

Another "creative craft" the Lord had me do was direct a single parent family ministry at our church. Now, why would the Lord place me in this ministry when I had been very happily married for over 30 years at that time? It is like God has created me as His "craft project" to be unique and useful at the same time. Where has God led you and what has He allowed in your life to make you into His beautiful "craft project", so you can be all you can be for His Glory and for His purpose?

Read 1 Peter 4:10-11 – When we are in alignment with God's will, there is nothing, I repeat, *nothing* we cannot do in His name. We can live a rich life of joy, contentment and victory. We can trust Him, no matter how creative He is with our lives.

Visions of Him – The next time you are gathering the supplies for your craft project, remember that He is doing the same thing in your life. Pray that you will become all that He wants you to be, to be used for His glory.

Deeper Visions of Him – James 4:13-17

Climbing Every Mountain

The other day, I was watching television and there was a documentary on a group of men mountain climbing. They enthusiastically described how involved the preparation was for such a challenging climb. They needed to get in shape so their hearts and bodies were strong. They needed to purchase the perfect equipment to set themselves up for success. If the quality of their gear was inferior, it could mean the difference between life and death. They studied all aspects of the mountain so they were prepared for a change of terrain or weather shifts. They could not leave anything to chance; their lives depended on it.

They headed toward the mountain with their minds racing and full of anticipation for the immense challenge ahead. Would they make it to their goal? What would it be like to stand on the top of the mountain and realize what they had accomplished? The moment finally came…with one foot in front of the other, their huge backpacks strapped on, they headed up the mountain.

This reminds me of the mountains we face in our lives. Some may seem absolutely insurmountable. Some may look like an easy climb. We can reach our goal to the top if we realize and rely on the Lord God to lead and assist us. Sometimes He may pull us, sometimes He may push us a little to keep us moving forward, and sometimes He lets us climb at our own pace. Sometimes He lets us fall, picks us up, and sets us back on track so we can reach our goal. We can prepare for the climb by using the right gear, which includes reading and applying the truth of God's Word, talking to Him and listening to His Holy Spirit, and taking one step at a time in submission to His timing and will.

When we are climbing our "mountain", He is at the bottom ready to catch us, beside us to cheer us on and at the top, and ready to receive us into His arms of love. No mountain is too high that we cannot conquer it with Him. You can know without a shadow of a doubt that you never climb alone, so be confident that you can climb every mountain that rises before you.

Read Matthew 17:14-20 – This story about the lack of faith of Jesus' disciples when they tried to cast out a demon in a little boy, caused Jesus to give them the greatest lesson about faith. Hide verse 20 in your heart today, claim it, and keep climbing.

Visions of Him – The next time you see a gorgeous majestic mountain, remember that no matter how high your mountain is, the Lord God is there to help you climb to the top, but remember that the preparation for the climb is up to you.

Deeper Visions of Him – Hebrews 10:35-39

Hold My Hand

Sitting in the airport, I watched as a little kindergarten-age girl followed her daddy in front of my husband and me. Her daddy seemed focused on getting to the ticket counter while his daughter tried to keep up with him. The man finally turned around and stretched his hand toward her and she ran to place her hand in his. She looked up at him, they both smiled, and they went on their way.

That same day, I also saw a two year old little guy who was being difficult and his mom was getting frustrated with him. She also stretched her hand back toward her son, but he stopped in his tracks, folded his arms and refused to obey. Eventually, after much coaxing, and pleading, his mom continued walking and the little boy began to follow a "safe" distance behind her.

Watching these two small children reminded me of our walk with God as His children. Our heavenly Father is always there ready to guide us and hold our hand, but we need to decide if we are going to let Him or not. Sometimes, we reach for His hand, while other times we fold our arms and decide to walk independently of Him. Just like that father, he had more knowledge of the possible danger ahead of his little girl, so he reached out for her. I am sure she felt more secure and connected once she took hold of that great big warm hand, and we would feel the same way when we take hold of the hand of our Father.

Why do you think we are not safe and secure when we refuse to take hold of that same hand? We don't know what lies ahead of us…the dangers, struggles or challenges, yet we think we can do it all on our own; but then we fall and wonder why. Walking close to God and holding His hand doesn't mean we won't stumble or fall, but God will absolutely be there to pick us up and help us move forward. Don't cross your arms, but run after Him and place your hand in His.

Read Isaiah 41:13 – Our security comes from our decisions to believe this verse with all of our heart and our will. Take His hand with confidence.

Visions of Him – The next time you see a small child holding their mommy or daddy's hand, envision yourself holding the hand of Jesus as He leads you through life.

Deeper Visions of Him – Psalm 63

Pumping Weights and Chinups

Back in the 80s, there were aerobic classes, dance classes and an overabundance of bright-colored spandex, knit leg warmers and sweatbands in every color of the rainbow. The "serious fitness enthusiasts" would go to the gym and pump weights, drink gallons of protein powder beverages and oil up their tanning-bed bodies to look "perfect".

I remember when the famous Jack LaLanne would stand in front of a camera in the 60s with his great big white dog, Happy, and do callisthenic exercises, which he continued to do well into his elder years. Then there was the crazy and passionate Richard Simmons with his tank tops, shorts and curly hair dancing to music and crying when he would talk about his past life of obesity. Following Richard was the infamous Jane Fonda in her striped gray leotard and leg warmers on a video tape that sold millions of copies…jumping up and down in bare feet and encouraging us to lift our knees higher and reach further.

The goal was to bring America to a higher fitness level and get us moving, and millions of us took the challenge and participated. Did you? Today there are endless types of classes you can join in clubs across the country. You can Zumba, step, bike, swim, pump, cycle, do yoga or Pilates, participate in ½ or full marathons or triathlons, or join a walking group. Shoot, you can even go to fitness "boot camp"! Millions of dollars are spent on indoor home equipment for those of us who would rather work out alone in the privacy of our own homes. Wow! We Americans are crazy about fitness, aren't we? Wait! Then why are we a country that struggles so much with obesity and complications from it? Hmmmmmm.

Let's look a moment into our souls. What about becoming stronger in our walk with Jesus? What would happen if we put as much time into our spiritual fitness as we do in our physical fitness? What if we made a strong resolve to pump spiritual weights? Would it lead us to being able to lift our chins with confidence and walk boldly forward in His strength and joy? We check out clubs and fitness groups and equipment, but what if we checked out resources to help us spiritually strengthen up in Jesus?

Read Isaiah 41:10 – The enemy wants to keep us weak and feeble in every way, but this verse is a promise from God that He will be our strength and uphold us no matter what we are going through. Do you believe Him?

Visions of Him – The next time you go to the gym and you look at those around you pumping weights and doing chin-ups, remember your need to not only build your "temple" up, but also your soul. His Spirit will be your Spiritual Fitness Trainer.

Deeper Visions of Him – 1 Peter 4:7-11

Forever and Always

What is your picture of what Heaven will be like? Do you see lots of light, golden walkways, mansion after mansion, or animals of all kinds roaming around? Do you see angels wearing white robes and playing harps with halos over their heads? Do you see God on a throne with a scepter in His hand and multitudes singing praises to their King?

When you look up and see white fluffy clouds with the sun peeking out from behind them, do you ever think about Heaven and that you will go there someday? Do you think you have done enough to get up there and live with God forever and always? Have you "paid your dues" here on earth and deserve to live eternally with Jesus? Have you been a good person, taken care of your family, tried to do what was right, even though you made some mistakes in your life? Is that enough?

Maybe your life has been a series of bad decisions and dark circumstances and you don't feel like you deserve to even imagine living in Heaven with the Almighty God. Maybe you don't even believe in the God you hear others talk about or you don't know what to believe.

Funerals, wakes and memorial services can bring our minds to thinking about such things as we honor someone who has died. Where did they go? Is this all there is or is there such a place as Heaven? Did they do enough?

The Word of God says that in order to spend eternity with Jesus Christ, we only need to believe that Jesus died for our sins and ask Him to become the King of our life. **"Believe on the Lord Jesus Christ and you shall be saved."(Acts 16:31)** That is it! It does not take a bunch of rituals, religious traditions, certain clothes, and a checklist of good deeds. God's grace and mercy, shown through the sacrifice of His Son, was enough. Here is how you can be sure of where you will go when you die. Please say this prayer and mean it from your heart.

SINNER'S PRAYER – *"I know I am a sinner and have done many things that do not please You. I need Your forgiveness today. I believe that Jesus Christ is Your Son, and that You sent Him to be brutally beaten and nailed to a cross to pay the penalty of my sins. Thank You for loving me that much. I don't want to live in sinful ways anymore, so I am inviting Jesus Christ to come into my heart and become my own personal Savior. Please cleanse me from all the sins I have committed. I need Your Holy Spirit to guide me in living for Jesus Christ the rest of my life."*

Visions of Him – The next time you look up to the sky, imagine yourself running on streets of gold in the freedom and joy of God. No more sickness, tears of sorrow, fear, or trauma in Heaven. You will live an eternity in His light forever and always! Hallelujah!

Deeper Visions of Him – John 3:16-21

Printed in the United States
By Bookmasters